PIANO · VOCAL · GUITAR

Days of Elijah

THE BEST OF
ROBIN MARK

ISBN-13: 978-1-4234-5297-3
ISBN-10: 1-4234-5297-6

HAL•LEONARD®
CORPORATION

7777 W. BLUEMOUND RD. P.O. BOX 13819 MILWAUKEE, WI 53213

Visit Hal Leonard Online at
www.halleonard.com

ANCIENT WORDS

Words and Music by
LYNN DeSHAZO

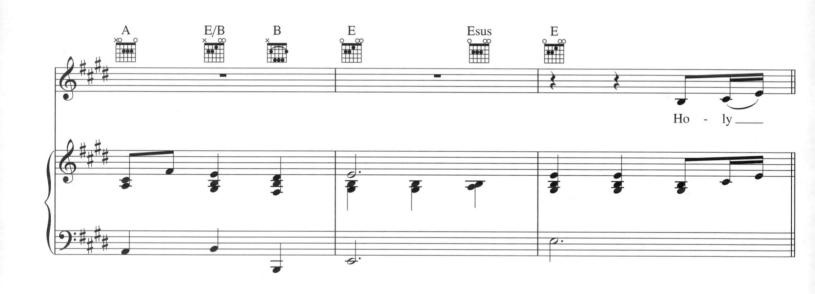

Ho - ly

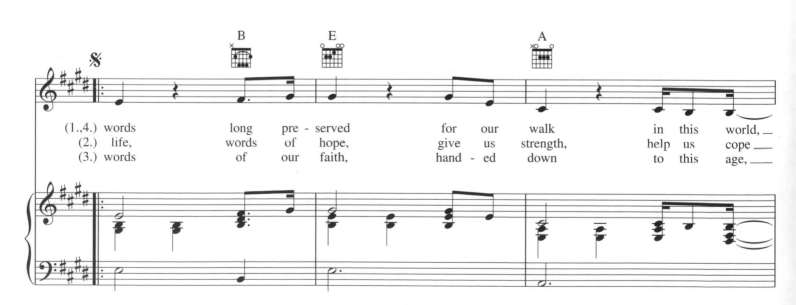

(1.,4.) words — long pre - served — for our walk — in this world, —
(2.) life, — words of hope, — give us strength, — help us cope —
(3.) words — of our faith, — hand - ed down — to this age, —

BE UNTO YOUR NAME

Words and Music by LYNN DeSHAZO
and GARY SADLER

Bm G D/F♯ A Bm G
Ho - ly, ho - ly, Lord God Al might - y, wor - thy is the
f
D Asus A Bm G D/F♯ A
Lamb who was slain. High - est prais - es, hon - or and glo - ry
Em Bm Asus A Em Bm
be un - to Your name, be un - to Your
1
Asus A
name.
2
Asus A
name,

DAYS OF ELIJAH

Words and Music by
ROBIN MARK

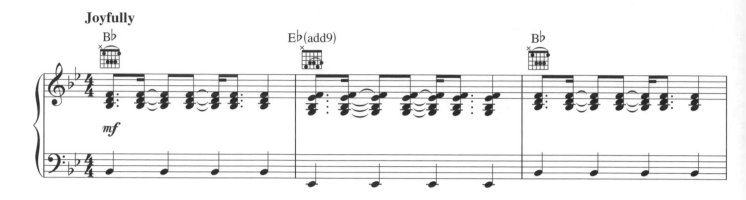

These are ___ the days of ___ E-
these are ___ the days of ___ E-

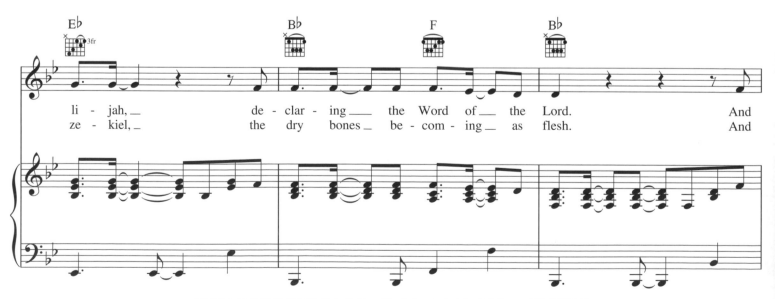

li - jah, ___ de - clar - ing ___ the Word of ___ the Lord. And
ze - kiel, ___ the dry bones ___ be - com - ing ___ as flesh. And

There is no god like Je-ho-vah, there is no god like Je-ho-vah,

there is no god like Je-ho-vah! _____ Be - hold, He _____

comes, rid - ing on the clouds, _ shin - ing like the sun _

_____ at the trum - pet call. Lift your _____

EVERYTHING CRIES HOLY

Words and Music by
ROBIN MARK

Moderate, relaxed beat

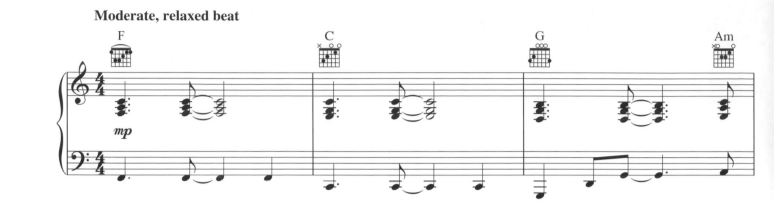

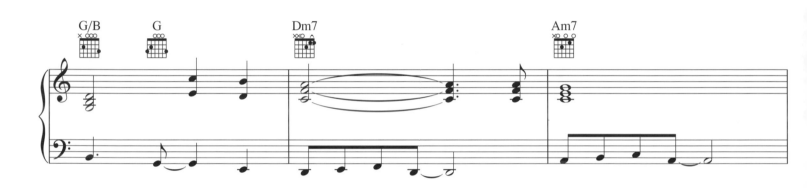

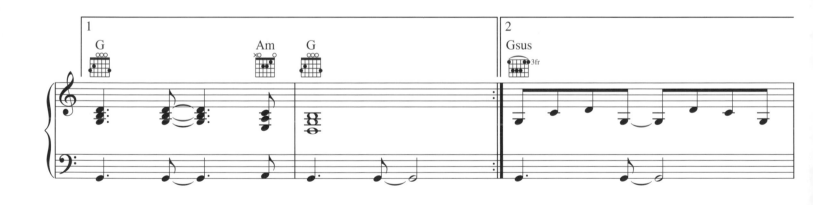

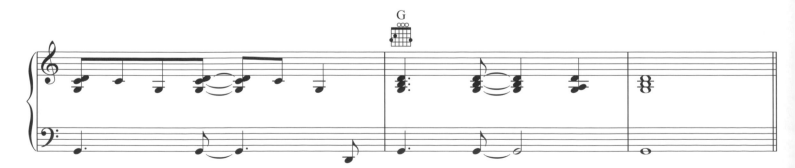

cast my crown __ be - fore __ You and bow down __ to pray. __

For ev - 'ry - thing __ cries ho -

- ly, oh, ev - 'ry - thing __ cries ho -

- ly, oh, ev - 'ry - thing __ cries ho - ly to You, Lord. __

HOW GREAT ARE YOU LORD

Words and Music by
LYNN DeSHAZO

Slowly, in 2

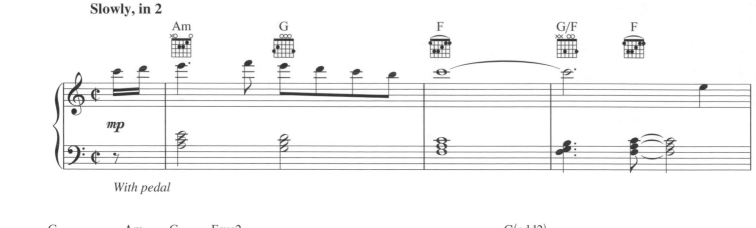

With pedal

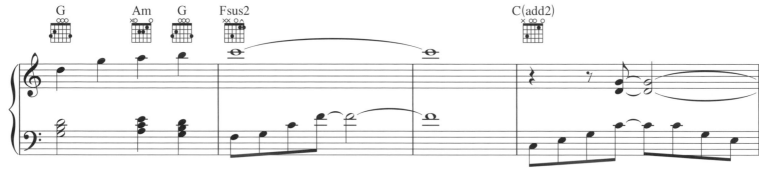

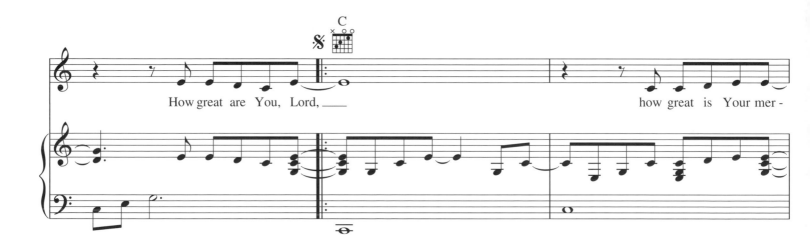

How great are You, Lord, _____ how great is Your mer-

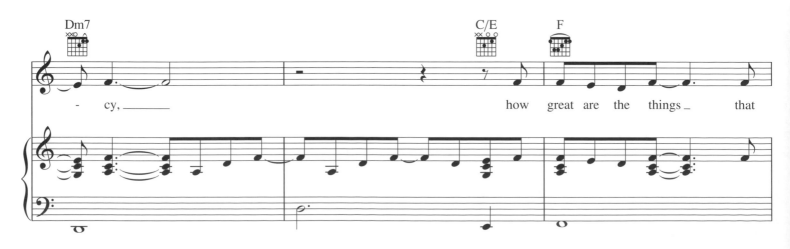

-cy, _____ how great are the things _ that

I HAVE BEEN CRUCIFIED WITH CHRIST

Words from *The Holy Bible, NIV Version*
Music by STEVE MERKEL and WES TUTTLE

who loved me ___ and gave Him-self ___ for ___

___ me.

JESUS, ALL FOR JESUS

Words and Music by ROBIN MARK
and JENNIFER ATKINSON

all __ I am and have and ev - er hope to be. __

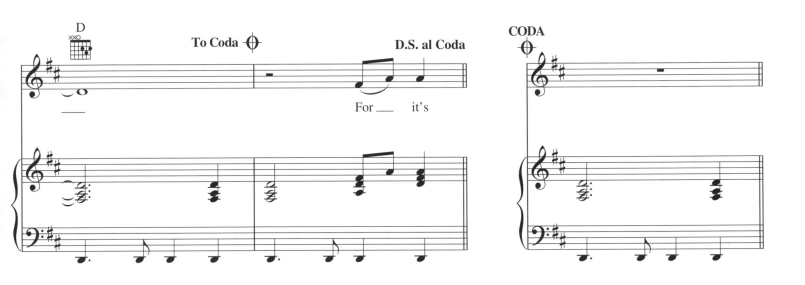

To Coda ⊕   **D.S. al Coda**   **CODA** ⊕

For __ it's

Repeat ad lib.

LORD HAVE MERCY

Words and Music by
STEVE MERKEL

With reverence

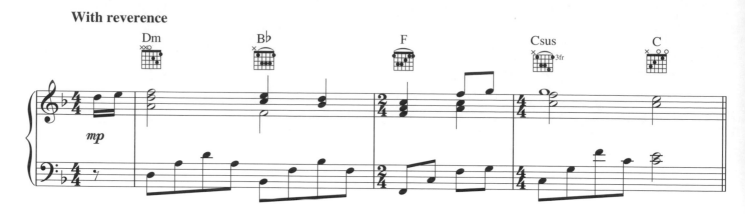

Je - sus, I've for - got - ten the words that You __ have spo - ken. __
I have built an al - tar where I wor - ship things __ of man, _____
I have longed to know __ You and all Your ten - der mer - cies, __

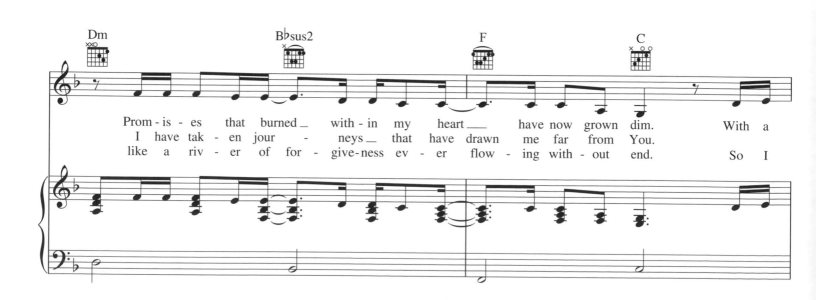

Prom - is - es that burned __ with - in my heart __ have now grown dim. With a
I have tak - en jour - neys __ that have drawn me far from You. So I
like a riv - er of for - give - ness ev - er flow - ing with - out end.

O AMAZING

Words and Music by
ROBIN MARK

Worshipfully

O a-maz-ing grace, how sweet
-ing love, how can
-ing God, the Fa-

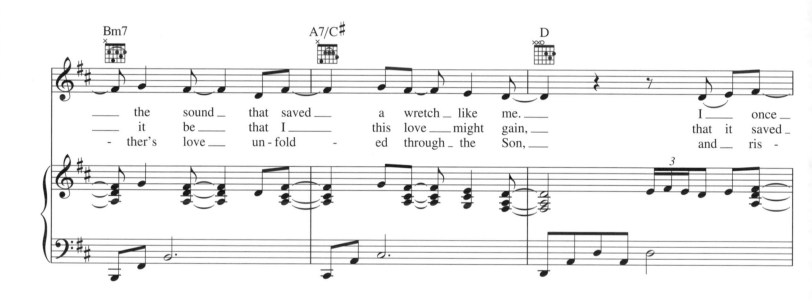

the sound that saved a wretch like me. I once
it be that I this love might gain, that it saved
-ther's love un-fold-ed through the Son, and ris-

was lost but now I'm found, was blind but now I see.
a help-less one like me whose sin had caused Your pain.
-en by the Spir-it's breath, the glo-rious Three in One.

REVIVAL

Words and Music by
ROBIN MARK

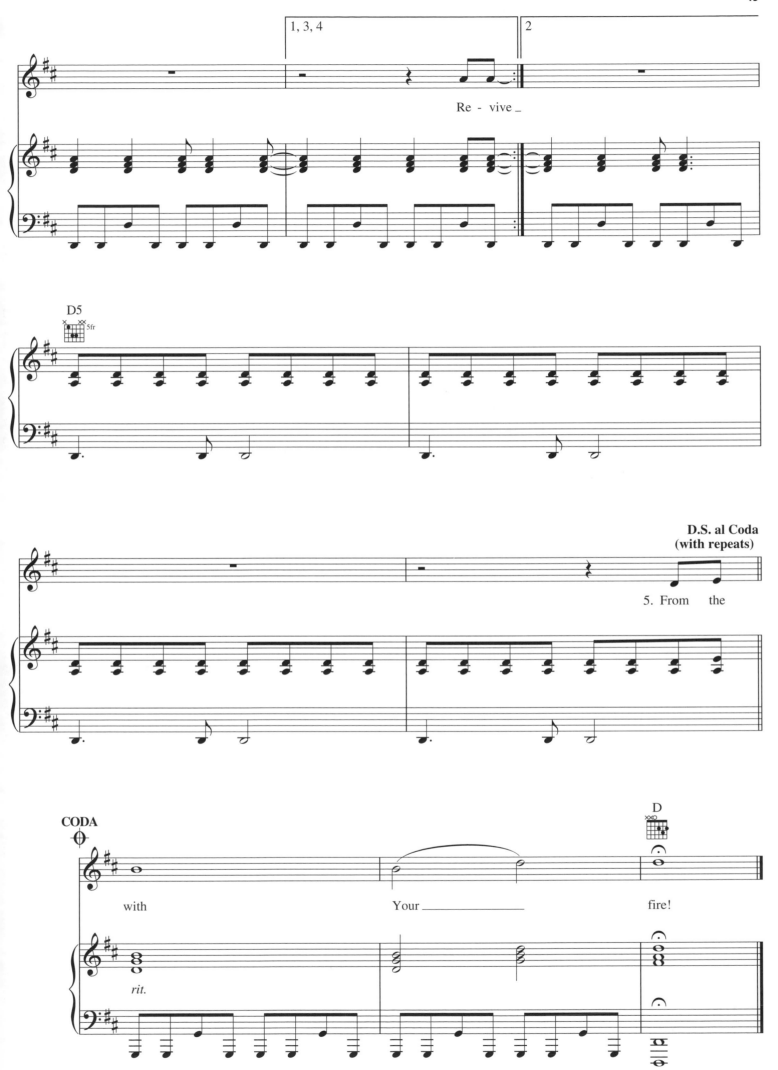

SHOUT TO THE NORTH

Words and Music by
MARTIN SMITH

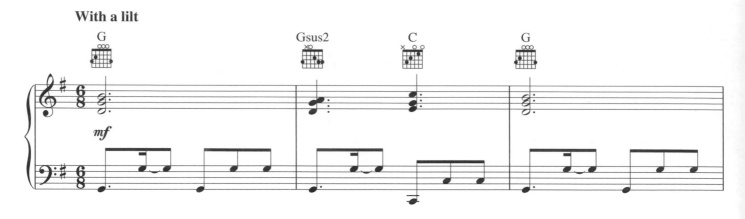

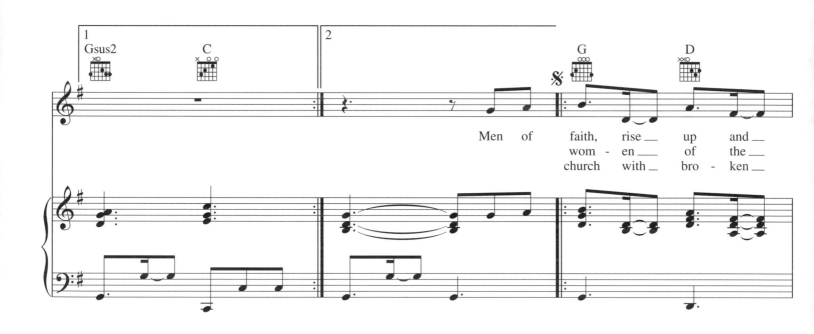

Men of faith, rise __ up and __
wom - en __ of the __
church with __ bro - ken __

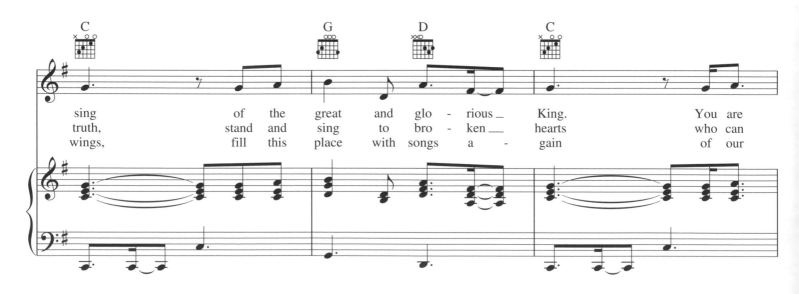

sing of the great and glo - rious __ King. You are
truth, stand and sing to bro - ken __ hearts who can
wings, fill this place with songs a - gain of our

WHEN IT'S ALL BEEN SAID AND DONE

Words and Music by
JAMES A. COWAN

THE WONDER OF YOUR CROSS

Words and Music by
ROBIN MARK

The won-der of Your cross ____ shall be our med - i - ta - tion,
To steal a - way at night ____ when they took down Your bod - y,
Were heav-en's prais - es si - lent in those hours of dark - ness,

© 2004 Integrity's Hosanna! Music/ASCAP
c/o Integrity Media, Inc., 1000 Cody Road, Mobile, AL 36695
All Rights Reserved   International Copyright Secured   Used by Permission

YOU'RE THE LION OF JUDAH

Words and Music by
ROBIN MARK

You're the

Li - on of Ju - dah, the Lamb ___ who was slain, You as -
shield in our hand and a sword ___ at our side, there's a

cend - ed to heav - en and ev - er - more will reign. ___ At the
fire in our spir - its that can - not be de - nied. ___ As the

THE BEST PRAISE & WORSHIP SONGBOOKS

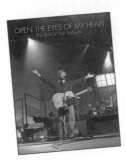

THE BEST OF PAUL BALOCHE – OPEN THE EYES OF MY HEART

This songbook features 12 of Paul's best praise & worship favorites: Above All • All the Earth Will Sing Your Praises • Arise • Celebrate the Lord of Love • I Love to Be in Your Presence • I See the Lord • Offering • Open the Eyes of My Heart • Praise Adonai • Revival Fire Fall • Rise Up and Praise Him • Sing Out.
08739746 Piano/Vocal/Guitar $14.95

THE BEST OF HILLSONG

25 of the most popular songs from Hillsong artists and writers, including: All Things Are Possible • Awesome in This Place • Blessed • Eagle's Wings • God Is Great • Holy Spirit Rain Down • I Give You My Heart • Jesus, What a Beautiful Name • The Potter's Hand • Shout to the Lord • Worthy Is the Lamb • You Are Near • and more.
08739789 Piano/Vocal/Guitar $16.95

THE BEST OF INTEGRITY MUSIC

25 of the best praise & worship songs from Integrity: Ancient of Days • Celebrate Jesus • Firm Foundation • Give Thanks • Mighty Is Our God • Open the Eyes of My Heart • Trading My Sorrows • You Are Good • and more.
08739790 Piano/Vocal/Guitar $16.95

THE BEST OF MODERN WORSHIP

15 of today's most powerful worship songs: Cannot Say Enough • Everyday • Fields of Grace • Freedom • Friend of God • God Is Great • Here I Am to Worship • I Can Only Imagine • Lord, You Have My Heart • Meet with Me • Open the Eyes of My Heart • Sing for Joy • Trading My Sorrows • Word of God Speak • You Are My King (Amazing Love).
08739747 Piano/Vocal/Guitar $14.95

COME INTO HIS PRESENCE

Features 12 beautiful piano solo arrangements of worship favorites: Above All • Blessed Be the Lord God Almighty • Breathe • Come Into His Presence • Draw Me Close • Give Thanks • God Will Make a Way • Jesus, Name Above All Names/Blessed Be the Name of the Lord • Lord Have Mercy • More Precious Than Silver • Open the Eyes of My Heart • Shout to the Lord.
08739299 Piano Solo...$12.95

GIVE THANKS – THE BEST OF HOSANNA! MUSIC

This superb best-of collection features 25 worship favorites published by Hosanna! Music: Ancient of Days • Celebrate Jesus • I Worship You, Almighty God • More Precious Than Silver • My Redeemer Lives • Shout to the Lord • and more.
08739729 Piano/Vocal/Guitar $14.95
08739745 Easy Piano..$12.95

iWORSHIP CHRISTMAS

Selections from the popular Christmas album, including: Away in a Manger • The Birthday of a King • Breath of Heaven (Mary's Song) • Come, Thou Long-Expected Jesus • Hallelujah • Joy to the World/Heaven and Nature Sing • One Small Child/More Precious Than Silver • What Child Is This? • You Are Emmanuel/Emmanuel • and more.
08739788 Piano/Vocal/Guitar $16.95

THE SONGS OF MERCYME – I CAN ONLY IMAGINE

10 of the most recognizable songs from this popular Contemporary Christian group, including the smash hit "I Can Only Imagine," plus: Cannot Say Enough • Here with Me • Homesick • How Great Is Your Love • The Love of God • Spoken For • Unaware • Where You Lead Me • Word of God Speak.
08739803 Piano Solo...$12.95

MERCYME – 20 FAVORITES

A jam-packed collection of 20 of their best. Includes: Crazy • Go • Here with Me • I Can Only Imagine • In the Blink of an Eye • Never Alone • On My Way to You • Spoken For • Undone • Word of God Speak • Your Glory Goes On • and more.
08739862 Piano/Vocal/Guitar $17.95

Prices, contents & availability subject to change without notice.

MIGHTY IS OUR GOD

25 beloved praise & worship songs, including: Above All • Firm Foundation • I Stand in Awe • Lord Most High • Open the Eyes of My Heart • Sing for Joy • Think About His Love • and more.
08739744 Piano/Vocal/Guitar $14.95

THE BEST OF DON MOEN – GOD WILL MAKE A WAY

19 of the greatest hits from this Dove Award-winning singer/songwriter. Includes: Celebrate Jesus • God Will Make a Way • Here We Are • I Will Sing • Let Your Glory Fall • Shout to the Lord • We Give You Glory • You Make Me Lie Down in Green Pastures • and more.
08739297 Piano/Vocal/Guitar $16.95

PHILLIPS, CRAIG & DEAN – LET THE WORSHIPPERS ARISE

12 songs from the 2004 release by this trio of pastors. Includes: Because I'm Forgiven • You Are God Alone • Let the Worshippers Arise • My Redeemer Lives • Awake My Soul • Mighty Is the Power of the Cross • and more.
08739804 Piano/Vocal/Guitar $16.95

PIANO PRAISE

This flexible book features 8 songs for performing in church as a soloist or at home for personal worship. Includes optional instrumental obbligato parts, chord symbols for improvisation, and a CD with play-along tracks and demonstrations. Includes: Firm Foundation • Jesus, Name Above All Names • More Precious Than Silver • Open the Eyes of My Heart • and more.
08739851 Piano Solo – Book/CD Pack................$19.95

VOICES OF PRAISE

10 worship favorites arranged especially for vocalists, including: God Will Make a Way • Here I Am to Worship • Open the Eyes of My Heart • and more. The CD includes vocal demonstrations as well as accompaniment tracks.
08739801 Medium Voice – Book/CD Pack..........$19.95

DARLENE ZSCHECH – WORTHY IS THE LAMB

15 songs from this contemporary worship leader, including: Blessed • Hallelujah • Irresistible • Kiss of Heaven • Let the Peace of God Reign • The Potter's Hand • Shout to the Lord • Worthy Is the Lamb • and more.
08739852 Piano/Vocal/Guitar $16.95

0606